Life's like Autumn Shade

Author of naming – WHEN I SAW THE GOD IN SAREE ,
SANITY-ZING, SOME PEARLS FROM STRING OF LIFE ,
DICTA TO GRAVY TRAIN , HOW TO GET ON VELVET ,
DICAT TO GRAVY TRAIN and more, Submissions of creative
entries in some of the most critically acclaimed anthologies like
THE BOOK OF 500 BEST POEMS by Authors Of India

Karan Sharma with holds an epitome of energy and spark in eyes to
change the world with his creativity and talent , which makes
various mentors and professionals spellbound.

His Podcast station "The Karan Sharma Show" is being streaming
on all leading platforms like Spotify , Itunes , Youtube etc.

Through analyzing the need to maximize connect with readers –
understanding the readership and catering to the reviews and then
try delivering best of the services , Karan launched his Online store
naming "The Karan Sharma Bookstore " in 2020 , which helped
readers get notified and grapple new titles as they are released.

He has been certified with certification of appreciation from
prestigious organization's such as UNICEF , WHO, AMNESTY
UNIVERSITY , GOOGLE and more on various courses of study.

With the selection and submission of Spectacular articles on
Medium.com , OnMogul.com Karan Sharma has marked his
footsteps to zenith inspiring alike individuals to whom opportunity
itself is looking for to grabbed upon ....

Poetries that sync like melody in life

Life's like Autumn Shade

*****

~moments and lives peoples and smiles~

~ ~ ~ ~ ~

Karan Sharma

To the Author ,

Please to know that you have such a talent and your words really touched me .

You have painted pictures with words and is each concept attaching itself to the next effortlessly .

Use of figures of speech; Similies, metaphor are superbly penned in your poems.

Well done !!

God blessings be upon you always .....

-Ms.Mamta

Vote of thanks – Glad to get such a great feedback , these blessings are what I work for , I reciprocate great wishes for your future aswell :)

Good Expression !!

Simple and Friendly language !

A blend of Roots and Branches of
Traditional and Modern.

Keep that up !!

-reader prefer to be anonymous

***

"Liked the steady hand, less grammar makes
it raw, and simple- and more humanly. I like
that.

Then, i see you're a great observer and have a
zeal for life. May be you romanticise life in
general.

I see you remember your achievements, even
as a young child. I like how you have
captured it in your words. Its justified to
compare your teacher's/parents' advice with
that of scriptures because both of these, we

realise their importance jab hum uss samay se Thora aage nikal chuke hotein hain.

It's funny- catering customers over the top. Are you comparing a professor with a shopkeeper, that's witty.

Chained in freedom adorned in every neck- makes me understand you're describing her appearance - in and out.

Chief of Bay- tbh i couldn't make much meaning out of it

I really like those 4 line of Books and shine- very apt

It's truly a great depiction of maa saraswati, really like it. Over all, so far, i appreciate the words you are using to express, not something one can understand by sole reading, really needs to understand each word to make a meaning.

Really don't agree to winter as gloominess tho-

Gorgonized- probably interested me the most

Let's go now, relive the way of nomad- that's genuinely a beautiful line. Genuinely like that

Come lets play with pencil and line- great !!

It is the epitome of Shiva, the one with dazzling diva- great rhyme- shiv ji sure impressed.

Keep faith, forget fake- very cool title for real

Alright so, all in all, i like how you're serving those thoughts in a tray.

There's variety in it, diverse- beautiful blend of traditional and modern- of roots and branches.

Something different for me-took me time to make meaning out of some"

-reader prefer to be anonymous

Vote of thanks – Magnifying the beauty in words , marking a more personalized note as a review about book was really enthralling. I took the review as a positive reinforcement and would try to be on your expectations in future projects .

***

They are great !!

Poems are too beautiful !

Great use of words and lucid language.

Clapping for you!!

-reader prefer to be anonymous

***

Its really Inspirational Writings .....

Some poems are really mesmerizing and was lovely reading them again

Really appreciate !

Keep it up, Blessings from my side !!

-Ms .Gaurika Sharma

Vote of thanks – Thanks alott for your
blessings , lead the path to this writer always
;)

***

To the Author ,

Its one of a Great piece which I came across ,
loved the depiction and soulful words .

Thank you Karan , I loved it !!

Keep up the good work !!

-Ms.Pritika Chugh (Co-Authored "Sanity-
Zing" , Psychologist)

Vote of thanks – thanks for showering your
sweetness on it , compliment your
humbleness –Thank you !!

Special mention – "The author is a young boy with potential to motivate people with his creativity. About the book it is author's first compilation of 19 poems. Roughly chronological in its progression, these vibrant poems collected in "When I Saw Godess in Saree" meditate on whole realms of poet's life experience. Mostly poems are short and reveals a depth of emotions 'life is like Carrom Strikes' and 'Regaining Chirps' in its symmetry of syllables, with its short-long, long and short lines punctuating poet's experience. In terms of form and language, the poems trend toward simplicity, utilizing direct language and figure of speech like use of alliteration in the lines 'Get awake you social animal.. Stop hyperbole havoc of your lethal cannibal.. Retain the karmic exponentially.. Profess, Propagate, Promote neutrality'..and short lines to let the empty spaces on their pages speak"

-by Dr Shivani Singh (She works as a, professor of Sociology in Amity University, Noida. She has spent the last decade in teaching and writing research papers. She mostly writes on women's issues. She has a very keen interest in reading and sometimes writing poems which gives her character a palpable spark.)

Vote of thanks – It's the readers which make my waves and ways –perceiving words with such great detail and beautiful sigh , I would bow to thank you for your such great insights and appreciating beauty in my work , will be waiting for your response in upcoming projects :) .

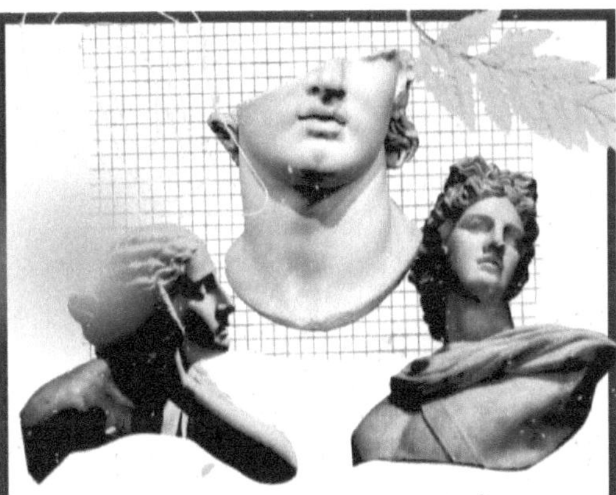

Just few lines on human beings

A being cluster full of emotions,
Happy to sad all are his notions,
Negative positive pros or cons
Ensuring the human beings to be ideal cons From tooth to
speakingwe are cross milestone
Shouting on the pitch in childhood ,
makes an adult with an understanding tone Moving a ahead
with a flashbacks helps to the individual
To hug the presentand forget the past and wait for the
futurewith dual aspect

Dedicated

In the lotus feet of my Parents and Teachers

. . . . .

HUMAN BEING : CLUSTERS OF EMOTIONS

This gracious piece is penned down by Honorable Ishani Chhaudha,(BBA LLB , LLM (IPR) . I am highly obliged for her contribution to this project.

Human beings are considered as full of emotions where every situation tends to depict how a human being is going through , every individual has its own way of understanding things , perception and handling the tenure of situations occurring gradually in individuals life , there is a saying called a motivation that keeps you going , i personally believe that inspiring minds always helps in tackling out the situations , for me life is just a like a train coming on the platform where every station decides the destiny of every passenger coming and going out on each and every place where the train stop , being an adult few flashbacks of my childhood

makes me feel happyhow enjoyable eating lunch with friends during lunch breaks was, how talking in between the classes and enjoying the games period was , then gossiping about every tiny torts with friends, wondering the little dreams of being an advocate , doctor or engineer or to be a homemaker too.
It feels as if I have just a few months back come to an adult stage where I need to be more calmand composed .

This shows how the changes of life and its situation helps in understanding which emotion should be drawn out of the treasure box that needs to be taken out , this is what mystery of life is when it gives you fruits of success it requires the hard work you paved for years .
These memories not only help us to recall the happiest moments of our lives but also help us to understand the sense of behaving in front of others or in society , because human beings cannot remain silent neither neutral that is were the values drawn in during the childhood

helps the individual to sustain the personal relationships with others , it is always said first impression is a last impression if the impression goes wrong the working will never be enhanced that is why it is always said that values allows an individual to remain in the human race which is full of good and bad things and life cannot favor on the good sides always it will make sure to have some sort of harsh reality of the practical world waiting for a hug from you always .

Betrayals , body shaming or any other xyz issues are also a part of this society but it is our responsibility to understand the essences on which actions can be taken , and just a smile always helps to reduce more stress. That is an impression of treating the right to others is always in your hands because you might have a worse time then also moving all the sorrowsaway. An idealistic approach helps in understanding a situation along with human beings andself introspection will ensure the path you took ahead of your life.

Preface

It is the 22nd year of the 21st century now , I am experiencing a 20 year of wear and tear that I have gone through – although a very short distance from the marathon of life covered till now, but the urge of me sharing some pearls of my writing which I through my conscience have penetrated till now and is now able to came forward to you in the hands of you as a podium by the medium of this book of mine, is something which provides me immense pleasure and great gratification about the journey I am onto.....

In this little initiative of mine I have managed to compile 20 years of my varied expressions , outlooks which I came across and would like to share with all of you - my fellow readers to get known about in a beautiful yet in a way which is enjoyable to read , that is ; in a poetry format .

The book contains 21 poems – 19 clinchers with one in completing and one for beyond ..... (19 poems and 2 poetic expressions) written by my upon different topics perceived under my sight , Hope you all like it and grace it with greater readership !!

With huge respect and great regard

Karan Sharma

Money and man one day ....

Once upon a time a tale got it tails
Curled upon adventure of creature which
started from caves
Crawled upon to corners now cabins which it
stays
Charm, cruel and creativity which adorn in
its plays

Man and money once got chill
Traveled upon sphere and climbed
up a hill
Looked around some shady looking
for same as sunny
With many honey and whole lot of bunny
Both wooed for honey - honey felt shy, some
got money other some time
Man married money , money with time
Moments of love , trust with some disguise

Man worked hard and lived with his life
Something worked with him some via her
prize
Both had a time which history bowed till
date

But some curtains fell before the show
Astonished , awake man realised its foe
Her life didn't followed to grave
Hands of other cheerfully she laid
Game of money with man tilled no trust
Balls of trust exchanged various courts , time
almighty makes lust to bust

Health's Heat

Eyes fixed forward which make life farther
Brain boxed to leave behind , protected
Smart tongue caped with enamels to bit
guilty
Good Health outshines every damn situation

Potatoes greased with mayo and castor
Beverages which counter every inner liner
Short-lived travel to which buddy gets
transfer
Clinics to banks which make him healthy
Good health is the key to every persons
wealthy

Fumes to sky and no drink water
Health awareness which needs to be cater
Needs and cries which hamper , after looking
to sky
Live happy with nutrition and diet , keep

afloat in marathon like a farther kite
Good health is something great in aspect ,
start from now or never it expect
Good for earth and good for life
Good health is ones better half as like wife

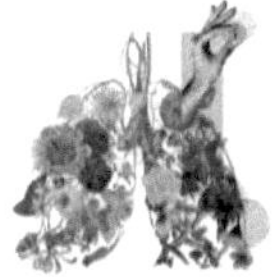

The Gold-digger life

Ploughing with sparkles of hope in disguised
Monotonous happy man seems to thrive
Digestion of dreams and for beyond he tries
Its the gold digger digging gold from the skies

With intense heat and pressure upon him
Solitaire solitudes bear the cold within
Ravages of time outsource his desires
Smiling wrinkles with wet his eyes , Doom to
dusk he is always in that lights
Away from the moon -to the sun he so strives
It's the gold digger life , of a gold digger cries

Regards to the nature and its laws within
Humanoid the heart of this century stealthin
Encroaching the beauty of souls within , its the
gold digger wife of a man within
He loves her to star and moon , it ditches so scar
to all the human goons

Hippie her life which prevails to happy ,man is

the one who ploughs to be happy
Barren on feelings and cold so emoticons , its the

life of a man who digs so gold -which digged his
goal .....

From the Gods Garden.....

Solitaire studded summarise I can
Like the pearl in the ocean
An oyster came to life I can
Angels from the heaven whom they pray
homage
Little disciple will always be on lonage

Stature of beauty , rejoice and chasm
Like the cold breeze on the sunny day -
relieved and calm
Chakra on the back of head that alarms
Bouquet of sunflowers which pose to this sun
all there alms

Like the saffron of life -which gave colour
and power
Insight to live , and lead at par

Words worth blunt for smiles of no scar

Melody to change and strive to be the best of
you are

Fairies   live on land
I saw one   so far

Fairies live on land I saw one so far .....

Paradigms ...

Crawling along the white n pure marble
Stepping stones to reach new marble
Marbles of joy from childhood enjoys till
now
Crunch and creme is not there now ...

Facets of faces are not unleashed till day
Gravity of emotions still prevail under tray
Books to worms still fascinate till today
Flowers need my hands to touch it still day

Stary nights with stars in life , bridges and
buildings still not a life
Love so rich , heart so poor -dominate no
rich neither one poor
Burrito of smiles and frappe of joys
Legit the things -which bib can't cover

Those where the days of computing less pairs,

those were the days of when prayers got cares

…

Pollen of heart .....

Chubby cheeks sugarplum smile
Glasses with black window to charm eyezz
Orchid face with mesmerizing plethora
Contagious smile , targettin the aura

Swanking none fluttering blunt
From butter to the cheese I saw a
garden of boutiques
Boutiques of flavours and awesome smiles
How can I get that larger teeth smile ??

Dimpled blushes rejoices , sublime and
serene
What I quote to the majesty n supreme
Sparkles to crown who's talks I say
Larger than life , not bigger than (age) me
what I state
I saw the vibgyor everyday .....

I saw the vibgyor everyday .....

Spice of life

Crave for the dish , water is in my eyes
Pinch of salt , tablespoons of rice
Cinnamon , cilantro to cardamom in every
bite
Sweet to chili life's essence in every bite

Pans of phases , stove of life
Ignited with love , nurtured for some childish
fries
Marination coaches life to be humble
Flavour and texture enhances life's bundle
With fire it cooks, but heart it melts
Sauce it serves , nurture it strives
Table makes staunch , but dining
makes it fine

Recipe of life -is secret to all knowns
Flavour , satire and pinch of salubrity

Cooked with eyes , heart and melody

Each-one is chefs daily so special

Need something in every proportion

Needs everybody in some of a proportion .....

Sun of my sky.....

From a little sapling of yours -now
under your sunshine is becoming a
plant.....
The leaves are green due to the pigment of
blessings you impart
Flowers and fruits feel overwhelmed under
you , fragrance of your charm ignites the "Be-
Unique" from one of you

Buds and full blooms are sparkling for gaze
Sparkling soul - sweetens every sour taste
Your praises on my books are something I
cherish for life
Enthusiastic smile I will forge and force
forever

Your imprints of valour and mist touched

soul and heart
Like the bee choose nectar , you made
honeycomb so far
Home to the future self I feel mystic in
disguise
I felt the magic of magician so of heaven

Gazed my sight I humbly surrender
Wizard in sigh who leads my path patting
together
Felt garland in my neck from the merry to his
child
Guess i had rubbed a lamp for long so ever
Making my god feel melody in life go ever

Chimes of him earlobed in forever ......

To Ever-shining Aura

– (Author of my life, whom I am disciple till eternity)

As white as daisy , white as Taj
Supreme shine of goddess which feel so large
Glaze in the eyes which are pints of perfumes
Guiding the little ones by essence so amuse

Name as peace and thy which prevails
Like the warm in the cold
morning , crystals which
humbly displace
Emeralds of the Chandelier
Flawless , Flamboyant persona
she adornes
Pinnacle of piousness , honour to the society
and patrons

First Teacher of life , teaching larger than
enlightenment that I am engross

May ur hand be upon this little ducks head
always for long
Its a prayer to this white swan , with rosary in
my hand
I offer my tears of joy in Gauri's feets on land
MahaGauri I am blessed seeing you daily as
heavenly garland

Mahagauri I am blessed seeing you daily live
as grand .....

Spectacular and serene .....

Spectacled spectacular charm who has
Contracts to the almighty who has
Agent on this land I saw the glitter eyes
Sweetner of life in real life

Composed Compost which is she enshrined

Exotic beauty in thoughts came to life
Brightest day in the days of life
In the shade of whom I felt god in disguise

Thanks to the temple in the sky
Rejoiced gentle mother advocate which
crafted by his dye
Exuberating ingredients of a holy persona
Learning makes engraves feels like sauna

Thanks for the fortune which I lay
Got such a great mother which my heart and
sould couldn't pay

Like the sandalwood smile......

Mapping down corridor with her gracious
aura
Serenity , sublime smile of plethora
Quintessential note of every Opera
In the feets of her humbly I possess my
obesiance

From the tulips of the almighty garden , a
lotus could be sensed
Essence of magnificiency , utter blessing to
the little bulbs she is

Words worth nothing whom I writing to

Mist of the angels -heavenly nector in the
words
Smiles and joy sprinkles in the sparkles of
footprints

Quicksand towards the best being she is
Bee humming blessings she is
Jewel scattering her contagious shine from
the almighty she seems
For this little fellow I could say for cent
I saw saraswati in feets down earth

I saw saraswati in feets down earth .....

Twigs of life .....

Its not like a bridgeway walk
Crossing in the city light , partner and
chauffeur
Wooing smiles and being beside needs nerds
to play with
Rajas to sit beside blasphemy drools kin

Its not a garden bloomers walk
Things take time and no talks
To mark belief and desires
Hold that smile and catch another liar
Furls of a rose it seems to stay -until the
pressure is applied to make essence a play
Stems and leaves stay as they are -cuddle of
beauty among stem play its part

Fruits are last to entangle one another
Flowers are some mischieves from era of
mother

From a sigh of a seed the plant becomes to
full bloom
But the bubble is burst when thoughts are in
doom
It isn't easy to add a soul
It takes time to change a roll - change ones
role
To sit beside a single seat soon
Suddenly pass to be a great boon

Its hard as brick and strong to build
Pasted and plastered , trusting every link
Kink of life starts to brush up
Smiles and sparkles lit to light up

Its becomes a bridge way utter a crest
Skyline flicker for Butter of the toasts as
pretext
Its hard to imagine and travel so utopic
Subject of a study who once was everyones
topic
Its hard to find and find to lose one
Wooing and smiles
aren't similies of
everyone

We live in hues

Like the autumn sheds sorrows of life
Like the spring borne the birth so wild
From Colours of clothes to colours of lie
I saw hilarious tye's and dye's

There's no reflection and no refraction
Beauty of nature is different in every
expansion
Lucid it May seem , seem it be
untouched
Live leaves breath , dead ones
crunch
Slippery on the floor of the soul so
drewed
People lie in blues like life is in hues
Life is in hues .....

There's no paint that colours it all
Some strokes fine to some strokes bold

I saw pervert flowing and diving gold
Gold diggers got saw gathering the gold

Even if its old and trees know the plunge
Deficating dedications and prevailing a purge
I saw some flowers felt shy waiting for fruits
into their tree
In the Bloats of ink and hues in trees
Views of hues are not to be undermine
No blank cheques are gifted everyday n time
But the palm also grow casting its part
Cater for the drools of so the heart
Dont make the music noise so harsh

Losing the melody -like a starless star

Like a autumn of flowers
Like the skin ashed in spring at last
We live in hues - whom not to do due
We live in hues -horns disguised as flowers
We live in hues -whom you not so apart

Unprece-tentative like upon this land.....

Human is stupid , cries and
to its surprise
Death is wise , and is not so disguise
To the shirt and necklace wear and tear
everyday
To the shoulders and brain- a souless string
paves it way
She doesn't shy , never it sly - caged man flyes
to sky
Rashes to ashes - this life is unsown
Turns of the lights , on record it start its play
Clapping and sighs - audience rehearses the
naive
Lights and honks - dress and satire
Freckles and wrinkles , bags of wisdom with
eyes
Life is a like what everybody thinks
Thinks and kinks sync this link

Its a brisk walk , castles of a cake walk

Eyes catch lies - smile worth no smiles
Life is a stepper of escalators
More I write - words change the lever
Its time sensitive -mix of thoughts
Might rot more than human try to sought

Death is like the timer of our race
Someone races - something sometimes
someones craze

Human is the piece of a die
Die of numbers , die of a cast
Casted upon a shadow this animal it chasm
Charms and chasm race in grains of chart

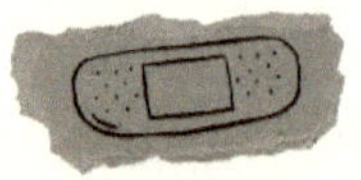

This is the bout of success in draft .....

When I am in the bout - its all they talk
about
Asphycxiating , excruciating the devil feels
loud
Cross walk , sweeting
every drop dem
drown
Rounds make him go
around by time

Falls to falls career by his sight
Sigh's of my punched face feel gorgeous
Lashed unleashed everlasts his tears like
canine
I made my cheque by thrashing this sign
Scumbags are some next in line
Make them beaten to sprang to the light

Its a day of life in the boxing bin
Goods of tin to somewhat sins
Alike alive a-lie's alias

Catch-phrased catch phases life such ways

Mice race of prestige that life chases

Let this bout be about you
You win by levels knocking versions of you
Be smile adorned always to light
Take curations into mind some lite

Heat is what makes u bake
Either it bake or brakes your take
Choose the knife wise as ice
Cool it to lake travelling a mile
Enjoy its journey not the
pedestal
Deal with the melt its
inevitable
Cater your takes on table
Blood which bleeds blends you to sky
Blurrs that bound spellbound your try
Persists precises the precision of craft
This is the bout of success in draft .....

This is the bout of success in draft .....

Chilledhood .....

Sky a canvas , parents my life

Crayons of life were free from force
scribe

Walked a mile without feel
hurt

Cry and craft was parcel of love

Gods my friends at every arena

Used to hold in hand who hold every hand

Mist of piousness was all that was round

Like the shapes dancing dangling around

Nothing was paid nothing too nice

I was solving the puzzles in this coming
puzzle life

Aura of rise , aura of smiles

Around me always was nothing of such
surprise

Even a leaf was a tree in self

Teachers were my best friends itself

Motherly charm I was beside so blessed

Surprising that i grew under shade of bearing
the suns

Small were palms , bigger were psalms

Met christ day to day in dreams so far

Love in the life was blocks and cake

Nor than todays block and taken takes

Leaves so left are are hard to find

Flowers once in bouquet are hard to remind

Walkers and candy's who's licious it was

Chill of life chills of grow

Child cries for the life full of cries that was

I never saw one such pure it was

I never saw one such pure it was .....

Tucked n Winged ..

Took upon a ladder to sky

To see such stars and staring the
earthy lie

Plasma mistic this ball seems

Layers of hands, positive , hold
it green

Unlike the hearts bottom out there

Its fresh and true

Its clean looks heaven who we dream down
to

Borders and boundary are concept such small

Small minds feel that shout

It looks like arms hugging a bowl

Bowl of fishes , mountains and soul

Thick green cover and iced chains from
above to down it grow

Deserts are not like the deserted sighs

Lakes are really like the hope of the eyeballs
which roll

This earth go round , move and change but
not so changed

Above its humble and quiet

Not like the noise and fake sight

Asteroids are here , even no breath

Value less penny this body is to the art , even
the soul has to depart

See this gamut of sparkle which u sow

Its lonely above but roots are from floor

Nice and kind is only currency to every door

Exchange of values , values you everything

Lets be the star one wishes for everything

Lets be the star one wishes for everything .....

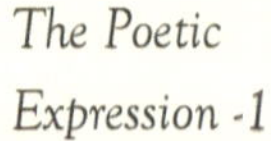

Ganga
and I

-   a drift of society and its beauty , an
    ugly makeup , a serene view , a scenic
    imagination , a timeless exponent , a
    breathtaking view to ones light , a life
    within lives , an ordained god .....

A flow that never ends ....

-a truth that never trends , scar
behind the joy.....

Ganga and I.....

The hums of navard rolling my eardrums ,
the seated silts of holy alta which mark steps
up the pave

I inhaled the vic and chants of a great ganga ,
the river of life ,a cottage in the industry , a
sheera after grind - like the hairs of mumma -
silk and sublime - wise as a child.....

Its dense and no desire ,churn of burbles
which pray , marks a parcel of mahesh ,
rajesh and sita

Ganga - syllables from the epiglottis , for
which the tongue feels relieved and lay

Splash of water hits the eyes , Shiv !! Shivi!!
Are u here - I got a cpr from a dream - a
dream that was a life of live -with difference
of its stage

Me with my younger buddie took a seem less sigh at the waters of great pride and bowed our presence by a namaskar .

With a monotonous smiles and greets from a height ashok uncle , lalu bhaiya and birju the phool wale bhaiya -I said harr gange and marked my steps towards the chaat paldi wala

.

Green chutney , aalo jhol and hot Kachoris in my disposable paper plate - "Goddess Ganga put my prays all in plate".....Laughed and gasped a sigh of hope that the blessings be there always .

With less then a foot and adjusting my feets by giving a way for passing cycle - welcome to my block its a Shiv alya .....home of shiva , paving way life the hairs of seer , quiet and cool without sunshine , the cool which has adorned in the minds of nerves near mine forever and for time .

Mumma Aaj Aaloo ka parantha !! Like a great savy , with denture plated with saliva which runs with undigested burps of kachori - its a mischief of me that maa ganga pulls my ear off - caught with every lie here and then everytime .

Cool verandha with open roof of sky that stores the breath of city in it , a place where birds fly -leaving twigs and wings as gratitude for being open skyed - in the phase of close roof and no open mind .

Dadu's stature which reminds of the city stalwart that stands directing ways , dadi churning the wheat by her gracious sight and glittery smile - calling and teasing her , distracting her from her so called work - I call badi amma (the big mumma ,used to state grandma) "tell me a story ones again na" , with no teeth and feeble voice -she says ohh my shiva , ohh bhole shankar -come , which story u want to know about .

Its a tough moment now , the story is always the same , same character and same end which its hilarious at times , but its tough , its tough seeing a window of life that has soo beauty in its brain , like the little flowers

draped all around the fabric of saree that
resembles maa amba at two blocks away .

Her say and sight is like the same prasada
that I get there for pray - but its tough to see
the hands of veins going too feeble , tears run
wishing for dadi's eternal as the gangas flow .

Next is my world personified -my mumma ,
views life larger like her eyes , smiles like the
openness of sky but cries and runs tears
sooner than the chaya aunties excuses for
work slyes (the helper of my world).

She is daisy of the garden , awake and adore
whom I admire before to my birth , she
makes the sky paint sunny even at my hazy
days .

Flowers , incense sticks , Jaggery and fruits
with Kumkum along a bamboo woven basket
- she hums my name "Shiva" along the way
everytime I join my little hand for going
Mahadev Mandir near home - I think she is
my fan or its one whom I remain blessed
getting kachori's for life !!

Like the metrocities machine counting stacks of dakshina , I have seen an ATM in Shiv Alya - it is male with 6 feet height , making it too high approaching to its top shirt pocket filled with the token to places everywhere .....

His smiles and praise is like sant vani , its like that I touch the door to heaven -the hardwork feels that shrugs off shoulders after the dip in ganga .

Sparkle in the eyes feel like the answer to the mantras chanted by bade panditji at ghat .

Bauji's gracious call towards pride in my name , feels sun braking its shower and shimmer in sky like a nectar in Panchamrita dripping in a pot of clay .

Beyond words my life has to say , below to it this shiva actually has to say .....

From shiva alya -a son of shiva writes this play .....to all the readers I am the one adorned by

god collecting the fruits from its statue of clay
- I am the one which can speak out of temple
but not from inside say - I can hear hums and
pray to it along I sweep the gulabs in the
sewage open around the dump .

With not so appealing sigh and friendly greet
I am the proud cleaner of humans shun .

Its the ganga and I which flow forever , same
bank (ghat) the foolish we cater leaving never

Its my fortune that god delivers me
segregating every leave of club(bel patra) -pray
of letter with me together.....

Its my shiva and I , its shiva of mine .....

"Whts
that
makes
the life a living ....." can

you hear meee !!

in this world full of shouts and noise, it's the drum beats , beats the symphony of whispers , the chimes of

sweetness, the

only tool that

overturns the

journey with

every flicker of

utter......

What's that makes the life a living .....

Seeing to a thing is like living (living for a moment or for in a moment)

But hearing is for life ....

It poses a great impact which gets etched in the memory forever

It has a mesmerization

A fact that talk can be a byscopic in nature - which according to ones ideas and notions hav its distinctive beauty in it

A sense that things can be seen and felt according to ones own perception , the words spoken are absorbing in nature - departs a deeper impact and has in trench value system that bein deep down help us reach our heart and soul

Visuals can be contemplative and somewhat
"artificial in the reality" of moment .

Whereas voice being an unstringed soul
marches to the voids and ties bringing closer
the sights of inner beauty

Proximity of being pragmatic and at the same
time being diligent in society communicating
convention , the words make feel the
emotions - the waves and the rush , the tides
of sweetness and desires , the jogs of anger
and cries

Voice envisages us keeping peace and pace at
the same grammer in the stretches of time

Its exorbitant rejoices that makes the heart go
round by listening to the various clocks
marching in the same moment of time .

Its a book of flavours , vibgyor that isn't dyed
, acoustic psalm that isn't died , that feel for
life and chasm to live is what the voice caters
for Matters for .....

life is framed

Painting a canvas takes scars and stains

Unplanned colours leaves impressions of
bane

Pints of paint go through pain

Ideas which adjust some window pane

Brushes dive down with humility

Perspective which perceives desires of
brewing pity

Its framed life

We cut the ties which make ones tongue tie

We lie to the ones who we perceive to lie

We adjust boundaries and make it frame

Hiding the surroundings to make it less lame

Moral of modern who's hypocracy only stays

Society slays by the minds of some which
prevails

Its sabotage and pity that human makes
words to cloth , loath its say

Frame of happiness decorate the hall in a
whole way

Streams of sad sits the soul -pierced the hole
way

Its walk of shame that we talk today

Live for frame that will be framed away

Body is on lease that will fade away

On face of which we swipe right n left

Will be framed with garland that no one sees
so

Change the strokes and stress on sizes

Streamline the sigh , making view more
widen

Friction isn't pencil which fades being brittle
while we write but is, a pen which uses
friction making sharpness to matters and lies

Its not the border which canvas - clay

Framing lies isn't way to find happiness in
grey

Its what should a man should see some day

Its what should a man should see some
day.....

How people sell

Gross the grass that is seeded in a play

Grey its arena which isn't that green to say

Strokes of brushes which paint this picture
no bright

Are sprayed and stained with human
lucocytes

Scented scapegoats who cried, to the ones
who cover their lies

Layed houses see house and
bodies of scar who digested
feekle brains of fake ties

Happiness there token of multiplying there
smiles

They managed to gift bullets who walked
bare feet for miles

Underground ideas of unfiltered minds

Underground things which they think they
like

Shadow of shames which they carry till die

Story of every divider this sigh

Its the love which bind the blinds

Love is fake when it makes sea of lie , love is
what makes u see no lie

See the desires and purchase no dreams

Soul says the truth beg you to hear that
screams

Let the eyes of brain see hindsight

No brainer feeding the limelight

Its the bait by wolves hired by lions so
disguised

Scoundrels scape this picture to demarcate
pry

Run for light which heart dont lie

Run for light which heart dont lie .....

Also by me

Co-authored by Psychologist Pritika Chugh , Sanity-Zing is a thin booklet comprising of compilation of articles dealing with steps to better mental health , toppling the taboo's related to mental health and leading a happy , joyous well being.

Also by me

A poetry book like never before - stitched and
sized with soulful illustrations , topics
binding from the length and breadth of crazy
childhood to wisest ages.....an enticing ,
enthralling compilation

Scan to explore the whole new world of Karan Sharma's newly launched application and other exciting stuff !!